# Introduction

Anxiety is a bear. A giant beast that might look cuddly and unassuming from a distance, but up close, it is really an unpredictable monster that will strike without warning. Claws and sharp teeth extracted, ready to fight. I should know. I was diagnosed with Generalized Anxiety Disorder over 25 years ago.

My journey with an anxiety disorder has been and continues to be challenging. I have wonderful days, and I experience not so great days. My aim here though is not to overwhelm by sharing my story, but to present you with my experiences. When we talk to someone who does not understand anxiety, it can be difficult to really communicate what is going on inside our minds and our bodies. Some simply will say, get over it, and move on. I truly wish it were that simple, and I am guessing you do as well. Others simply do not understand what it is like to face this bear and to struggle on some days with emotions that simply do not make any sense. To experience feelings and thoughts that overwhelm us to the point of exhaustion. To have a desire to self-medicate and escape the world. But I understand, and totally get it!

My understanding of what you might be experiencing was the impetus for writing this book. It is my hope that this information will help you in some way, even if in a small way.

As with some books on anxiety, this is not a book about how to treat this disorder, or how you can live an anxiety-free life. This is my account of my challenges and victories over the last 25+ years. I believe that we are shaped by our experiences, and when these experiences can be shared, we learn. Recall a time when someone shared a great story with you. I am certain that you walked away from that interaction with new light, a new way of looking at things. That is my goal here. It is my hope that through these pages you might see a part of yourself or someone close to you.

You might read something and say, yes, that sounds like me or that is a great way of looking at this. When we identify with something learned from another, we can begin to see ourselves and maybe make a change or discover something new about ourselves. Maybe my challenges and victories will help you find something new about yourself.

Before I begin, I would like to outline a few essentials. First, I am not a licensed clinician. I do have a PhD in Psychology and have been working in this field for over 25 years, but I am not licensed. I think it is important that you know this tidbit of information mainly because I am transparent. I want you to know who I really am. I am just a person who has an anxiety disorder, who is trying to live honestly and without judgment.

I do have professional experience in helping those

with anxiety disorders, stress-related problems, and

addictions. Currently though my work is strictly as an

online professor. I love what I do and in some small

way, it allows me opportunities to share this wealth

of knowledge I have inside my brain with others.

Honesty, integrity, transparency, and a helpful soul is really what guides me today. I love having conversations with others, sharing experiences, and just letting things flow. When I decided to write this book, I wanted to provide not only my experiences, but to do so in a way that was open and honest. I do not blow smoke, and I am direct in my communications. My intent is not to judge or be overly critical of anything or anyone. I am opinionated when it comes to human behavior though, but it is based on psychological fact. I use the term "fact" loosely. In psychology so much of what we know is based in theory, and our behavior is driven by so many factors. I am not writing a textbook here, so theories aside, I just wanted to share my truths about anxiety, and yes, I may say a few clinical things here and there, but those are just

added for substance.  I want you to know the truth

of my challenges, and to learn who I am, anxiety and

all. Through these pages, I hope you can find

something that will help you and maybe allow you to

look at your anxiety and your life in a new way.

# The Beginning

I was not born with an anxiety disorder, nor do I believe that we are born with any disorder. I believe we are created through our environments, our interactions with others, and our worldviews. We see something when we are young, and we internalize it. Over time, this becomes who we are, and how we cope.

For all the biological supporters out there, I would argue that yes, there is a biological component to mental health disorders, but these are not the only consideration, nor should they be. There is no history of anxiety disorders in my family, living or otherwise. Therefore, my anxiety disorder was created not within a genetic code, but rather through my experiences and what I internalized.

What did I experience as a child that might have developed into anxiety later on? I cannot say with any degree of certainty. Maybe all of it, maybe none of it. If none of it, then why even bring it up? I can answer that. Because it will help explain who I am and why I behave the way I do. After all, we are all the sum of every experience, every thought, and every emotion we ever had, so in a way, my childhood and upbringing can influence who I am today, and how and why I developed this disorder.

This little trip down my memory lane will be brief. Trust in the fact that I have analyzed, maybe over-analyzed my childhood to the point of saturation. From birth to six years of age, I lived in Maryland. A very small town, with small town values. My father worked, and my mother stayed home, and I am the youngest of three girls. I would go so far as to say the development of my formative years was normal. I went to kindergarten, played with my sisters, and shared meals with my family. Normal.

In 1970, my father transferred to Las Vegas, Nevada. He worked for the government, and there was a job there waiting for him. So, we moved across the country. I think this little journey was harder on my parents. As a kid, you just go where you need to go.

I lived in Las Vegas from 1970 to 1990. From six years of age to 26 years of age. The early part of those years was again normal to a certain extent. I am not sure even to this day, if life in Vegas is what changed me, or if it was something else. But I will share that life in Vegas did change my family overall.

One sister did not adapt well to the change and was rather shy and introverted. The other sister was outgoing, had lots of friends, and was quite popular. I was neither. I had friends but I was also quiet and shy. I do recall though that when there was tension in the home, my role was to lighten the load. I know now that I was the family mascot. I disliked tension or anything that disrupted the normal day to day. When I would sense this, I would make a joke or say something to distract from the uneasiness.

The family tension was centered mostly on my two older siblings. They fought a lot and when I think about this today, it really was no surprise. I think in some way, they were envious of each other. The quiet one wanted to be more outspoken and popular, and the outgoing one wanted more solitude. Just a theory of mine though. What was real about me was the mascot role. I loathed stress and tension and would do whatever it took to lighten the load at home. This part might have something to do with developing an anxiety disorder later on. My aim was to please others. My goal was to show others that we should laugh more and cover up our emotions with a joke.

Life carried on this way through high school, and after I graduated, I started college. I attended the University of Nevada, Las Vegas, with the goal of completing my bachelor's degree in business. I had no idea at that point what I wanted to do in terms of a career, so I went to classes and had fun. It was college after all. I was an 18-year-old freshman, and there were plenty of opportunities for socializing and actually falling in love for the first time. It lasted one semester.

I realized that my desire to please others
and reduce tension carried over into college life,
and I would have done anything to be liked and
to put others needs in front of my own.
Especially by the person who I fell in love with.
When he graduated, he was going to move to
Southern California to take a job at an
accounting firm in Los Angeles. It was a big deal
for him, and I know he had to go. But
emotionally, I was a wreck. I tried all kinds of
ways to get him to stay including threatening to
hurt myself and feigning pregnancy. None of it
worked. Of course, it didn't work. He was not
thinking about me naturally. And I was not
thinking about him. I was more concerned with
the conflict within myself and how I was going

to reduce these uncomfortable feelings. I felt rejected, hurt, and deeply saddened. If you are keeping track, this might have been a catalyst for developing an anxiety disorder.

After that first semester of college, my boyfriend asked me to move in with him and move to California. I was ecstatic! Naturally, I moved in with him and uprooted myself to Los Angeles. It was fun but I found myself trying too hard once again. I was here in California with him, now how was I going to keep him? How was I going to encourage him to take the next step and marry me? I can say this now, but silly me. That's not how this works!

We grew apart and after about six months, I moved back to Las Vegas. I attended a community college, took a few classes, lived with my sister for a time, dated a lot, and just lived my life. I was able to overcome the sadness of the loss of my one true love by dating many different men. Let me emphasize, many different men. As a people pleaser, and someone who loathes conflict, one way that I learned to be accepted by men was to have sex with them. Wherever, whenever. Men were the guiding light to my feeling respected, loved, and cherished. They took care of the negative feelings I felt inside. I had value and acceptance from others; I was worthy as long as I was having sexual relations with them. Okay, now I think we can make the proverbial leap of faith

here, that this mindset can set one up to develop

an anxiety disorder. But there's more!

# 1984

This is not a chapter on Orwell's dystopian vision of society. It is a chapter on what I believe to be the true catalyst for the development of my anxiety disorder. Before I continue, I want to add a few words about causes or development of mental health disorders. There are many, many reasons why a person might develop a mental health disorder such as generalized anxiety or major depression. The reasons are as complex as each of us.

In my business, we typically look through the lens of what's called the bio/psycho/social model. This means there are biological, psychological, and social factors that can contribute to the development of a disorder. Remember, there is nothing absolute about our psychology! Each of us will view the world differently, remember things differently, and process information differently. Our thoughts, feelings, and behaviors being as unique as we are. I think also there are some factors that are more likely to influence the development of a disorder such as childhood abuse, trauma, or substance abuse. But again, no absolutes! If you wish to find the causes of your anxiety, you will need at some point to take a deep dive into your psychology. More on that later.

In terms of causes though, I would like to emphasize that I am not referring to blame. Blame is a separate animal, and I at no time blame anyone or anything for my anxiety. And I do not need to know the cause of something in order to treat it. If I have indigestion, I take an antacid. Do I know the cause? Possibly the bad pasta I ate, or it could be something else. All I know is I need to treat the indigestion. For some folks, finding the reasons behind something are important. If this is you, then great, take that deep dive and find the cause for you and you alone. I prefer to know something about the cause because maybe on some level there is something there that I need to look at further. Other times, I just know I experience anxiety and know I need to act.

The following chapter or two is only my interpretation of events that *could* have influenced the development of my generalized anxiety disorder. See above for clarification. Again, I use the term "cause" loosely.

In 1984, I started using cocaine. As a people pleaser, I wanted so much to be accepted and liked. When I was first introduced to this white, powdery substance I had no idea it was a game changer, but what did I know. I was 21 years old and very naïve. I just wanted to do something other people were doing. It was the 80s after all and cocaine in Las Vegas was everywhere! Couple that with a desire to be liked and accepted.

Over time and with continued use, I developed an addiction to cocaine. I think this occurred sometime in 1984 because I do remember quite well that in 1984, I started doing things that I would not have normally done. You know that behavior of an addict where the lines of doing what is right or doing drugs are blurred? Oh heck, let's be real. The drug was way more important than anything or anyone.

Enter 1985, and I was up to 3 grams of cocaine a day on a good day, and only 1 gram on an okay day. I was working so I had money to buy the drug, and again, it was Vegas in the 1980s and drugs were in most workplaces too. I even worked in the same restaurant as my drug dealer! Does not get much better than that.

When money was tight, I found other ways to secure funds, and those details will be left out. If you or someone you know is or was an addict, you know what I am referring to and that is enough for this book.

I abused cocaine from 1984 until 1991. The seven years I refer to as the first seven years as well as the "dark times." I do not remember much of the day-to-day things that went on, but I do remember the fun times. Yes, there were fun times. Heavy metal was big in those days, and along with my hairstyle, leather, chains, and cans of Aqua Net, I was into it as well. Friends and I would travel on buses to see bands in Arizona or California, and it was just fun. We would drive to California just to visit the Sunset Strip to see all the bands. If you were part of this scene, it was fun, wasn't it? Unfortunately, for most of us, these days are all but a memory. A memory though that I believe still crosses my mind now and then, particularly as it relates to

my anxiety. Although I do listen to Hair Nation
on Channel 39, Sirius XM Radio.

See, drugs, and alcohol allow us to forget
our feelings. Those 7 years were really about
covering up anything negative that I felt about
myself. In essence, the drugs did their job! But
there was also something else that I used to
cover up my true feelings. Gambling. Along
with abusing large amounts of cocaine, I also
compulsively gambled. I mean what else is a
person to do who cannot sleep in Las Vegas?
Seems almost natural.

In late 1989, my sister, who had left Las Vegas and moved to Orange County, California, told me that if I stayed in Vegas I would either be homeless or dead. I am not sure if I believed her, but I thought about it. I mean living in Southern California would allow me more opportunities to live the heavy metal lifestyle. At least the drive to the Sunset Strip was shorter!

In January 1990, I left Las Vegas and moved to Mission Viejo, California. I left with very little money, one cardboard box full of clothes, and my Guns and Roses wall hanging. On some level I knew my sister was right. I was strung out and oh so very tired. Being an addict is work!

I had managed to stay off drugs for a time in California. But in 1990 I went to work for a company in Irvine where drugs were available. I met my new best friend and reclaimed my other relationship with my other friend, cocaine. My friend knew how to get it, and for me it was like no time had passed. I felt normal again. I even found ways to travel to Vegas to engage with my other friend, gambling.

Life went on like this for a while. I

worked a few jobs, had friends, and met my first

husband. In 1991, something changed in me

though. Some addicts call it a moment of clarity,

but I refer to it as my spiritual awakening. I used

cocaine for the last time on December 22, 1991. I

am not sure how or why I stopped, but I did. I

just felt like God had spoken to me and said, quit

or die. Obviously, I chose the former, as I am

here today sharing my journey with you.

Following the cessation of cocaine, my physical and psychological systems went through a few major changes. I do recall such deep feelings of sadness. I was not high any longer, so now when I look back, I think that is natural when one stops using a large amount of a stimulant. But there were other physical and psychological changes.

I had my first panic attack in a bowling alley of all places, and to this day, I am unsure as to why I had this experience. Make a note here though that any addiction covers up our emotions. Without drugs or other behavioral activities, the emotions need to do or go somewhere.

Back to the panic attack. All I remember was this overwhelming feeling of dread. It is so difficult to articulate this feeling even today, and I believe that unless you have experienced this feeling, you cannot understand what it is like. Like the walls were closing in and I had no way to escape. It was fear, dread, uncertainty, panic, and just pure terror all rolled in a tiny ball that was consuming my mind and my body. I ran outside to catch my breath and after a few minutes, I started feeling better. And after that experience, I noticed that I also started to have difficulty being in enclosed places. Are you starting to have the a-hah moment? I can feel it today even as I am typing these words.

I did not have any further panic attacks after the bowling alley, but I did notice other changes like feeling excessive energy for no reason or feeling like my body was stressed. Racing heart, labored breathing, or just keyed up on certain days. I was working for a Navy contractor at the time in Anaheim, California, and remember not being comfortable in our conference room (it was too small for the number of people in the room), or always needing to sit by an exit. It soon became my norm. Just sit by the door. If you have bad feelings or another panic attack, just say you need to use the restroom. For the next six months this was my norm until something happened in March of 1992.

1992

In 1992 and without sounding overly dramatic, my world changed for the first time. I was still working for the Navy contractor in Anaheim, and I started going to school. My goal was to get my bachelor's degree in psychology. I did enroll in school and began the journey of my life in this field. But in March 1992, I started noticing that I just did not feel well physically most days. I was tired, nauseous, and my right side hurt. I was out on a walk with a friend this particular March afternoon and told my friend that something was not right with me. I just felt so sick. Keep in mind that my physical and psychological systems were still adjusting to not using the drug. I had been clean for only about three months, and in some circles, this is not a very long time.

I went home from my walk and the pain and nauseous feelings got way worse. I started vomiting uncontrollably, and the pain on my right side became so bad that I could barely walk. I drove myself to the ER (not sure how), and after a myriad of tests, they found nothing wrong. Or so I thought. The doctor who was treating me said, and this I remember clearly, I am worried about your white cell count. It is very high, almost too high. I am going to admit you to the hospital for further testing.

After two days of tests, I was diagnosed with gallstones. Amazing how something so conceivably small can wreak havoc on your body. In the 1990s and the age of HMO care, the doctors decided to not remove my gallbladder. The gallstones were manageable through diet or so they told me. I was released and told to stop eating anything with fat and to not drink alcohol. I did not have a problem with the alcohol part, but how was I going to give up fat in my diet? Suffice it to say, it was either eat a cheeseburger or be in excruciating pain. I chose a fat free diet.

At this time, nonfat foods were the thing, so I indulged with fat free cheese, fat free hot dogs, loads of salads without dressing, and fat free Snack Wells. There was still some discomfort, but I was okay. After losing about 30 pounds, I decided that I could not go on this way. I started to increase my fat intake just a little each day to see what I could tolerate. Over time, this new diet of some fat caught up with me. I ended up back in the ER, lying on the floor, curled up in a little ball. The pain was so bad I could not even stand up. I have been told that this pain is similar to giving birth. I don't have children, so I don't know about that. All I knew was this pain was unbearable.

After the ER visit and a subscription for pain meds, I visited my doctor. This was May of 1992. I told him rather forcefully that I needed to have the gallbladder removed. I don't care about your thoughts on controlling this with diet, or whether my insurance would cover the surgery. This thing was coming out and it was coming out soon! Clearly my assertiveness worked, and I was scheduled for surgery.

On May 25, 1992, my gallbladder was finally removed. After a couple of weeks of recovery time, I started to feel normal again. I started up with school again and for about six months my life went on with work, friends, and school. At some point I am certain you are wondering about the anxiety! Well, here we go.

Allow me to back track a bit. Trust me it will make sense! Following my gallbladder removal surgery, I woke up in the recovery room feeling intense panic. But this panic was different. I was flailing my arms screaming for someone to help me. I felt like I had died in surgery, and no one was coming to help me. Then I woke up from the anesthesia. Apparently, coming out of the anesthesia elicited some weird dreams about me dying and no one saving me or even trying to help. This is the incident that I believe started me on the path to my anxiety disorder. All the other things that I had experienced up to this point were also foundational in my development of an anxiety disorder, but this experience has been noted by some professionals as the one catalyst.

During a class in late 1992, I was sitting in my chair at my table, and the panic returned. The impending doom of another panic attack, where the walls are closing around me, and I need to escape. But I cannot escape because I am sitting in a classroom with 30 other students, and I am far away from the door. In fact, I am in the middle of the room. Where was my escape? Am I to run for the door quickly before anyone can say anything, or just sit there and let it pass? I am not sure if you know anything about willing yourself to not feel a certain way, but I tried so hard to sit there in my chair and talk myself out of this panic. I knew others were watching me, because I was acting kind of strange, but no one said anything. Then I realized that if I were to get up and leave the room, everyone would be watching me. I did not know which was worse.

After minutes which seemed like hours, I decided to

get up. I whispered to the student sitting next to me

that I had to use the bathroom. I left the classroom

and just wanted to be outside. I waited until class

was over to collect my things and explain to the

professor that I was just not feeling well. No harm,

no foul.

School continued this way for me until I graduated with my BA in Psychology in late 1994. I did learn though to always sit near a door, and to avoid situations where I was in the middle of the room surrounded by people with limited means to escape. It's rather funny now, but do you know that no one cares if you get up? All that time I spent obsessing over what others would think of me if I had to get up during a class. And I mean obsess. Prior to the start of my courses, I would find out which classroom they were going to be located. I would then visit that classroom to determine where I would sit. I knew every exit and I planned out my exit route. What I loved the most were classrooms where the professor was in front, and there were lines of tables. And the back row was near the door! I did become rather a back row person and to some

extent, I still am. Still searching for my escape route.

Prior to graduating with my bachelor's degree, I had also decided to work in a different field. I really wanted to work with people and leave the business world behind. I did take my first job in the human services field and left my great paying job to work in a group home for $8.50 per hour. I would find a way to make it work financially. I worked hard at this group home and was promoted several times within a matter of months. In essence, the change financially did work. I was less anxious too except once again, when I had to be in groups of more than five people where escape was in question. But working in a group home was a rather busy place, so being enclosed was few and far between. Most of the time I was outside playing with the children, or in groups of one or two persons. I carried on and it was business as usual. Just had to ensure that wherever I

was, escape was possible.

1995

In 1995, I started to develop gastrointestinal issues. Did my gallbladder grow back? What was going on? I was experiencing diarrhea after eating, and it was not pleasant. No matter what I ate, I had to use the bathroom right after I ate. And I mean right after. This went on for six weeks. I had lost more weight, and I could not figure out what was going on with me. I know six weeks is a long time to have this problem, but I was certain it was just stress. After six weeks though, I went to the ER. They did their usual tests and ordered a colonoscopy. They found nothing wrong and attributed the diarrhea to stress.

I was still working for the group home in 1995 and formed a friendship with the house therapist. We became very close, and after many hours discussing our problems, she said I should see a therapist. She believed that my stress and anxiety were related to the trauma of my gallbladder surgery and feeling like I had died, and no one was there to help me. Was that really a trauma? I had always thought that trauma was something way worse like a car accident or the sudden death of a loved one, or even abuse. My surgery was not trauma, but I decided to heed her advice and see a therapist. I chose a psychologist that specialized in trauma, and we had our first session. This was really a game changer once again!

My therapist had informed me that trauma can be perceived differently by each person. What one perceives as traumatic is different for each person. He validated that what I experienced in recovery from surgery was traumatic, for me. I was helpless and felt no sense of control. That can be traumatic for anyone really.

This really opened my eyes to how the mind works, and how what is for one person may not be for another. I think this also furthered my interest in studying psychology and helped me to understand how vastly different we truly are. Something I still hang on to.

After a few sessions with my therapist, I was diagnosed with Generalized Anxiety Disorder. I had a name for what I had been experiencing, which in a way was a relief.

Diagnosis and Beyond

After I read up on the disorder outside of the therapy room, it did make sense. Generalized Anxiety Disorder or GAD is characterized by excessive worry. And who had worry? Me! I worried about the physical symptoms, the diarrhea, the where to sit so I can escape worry, the worry about what others thought of me, etc. There was so much worry in my little world. There are other areas that encompass GAD like not being able to concentrate and feeling keyed up most of the day. This was also me! I also experienced symptoms related to anxiety such as heart palpitations, dizziness, and rapid breathing. And my feelings were pervasive. This is important because I experienced anxiety everywhere—work, school, home, and even in social situations.

Now that I had the diagnosis, what now? My psychologist wanted to try something called Eye Movement Desensitization and Reprocessing or EMDR. Maybe you have heard of it? I asked loads of questions about this approach and was provided very thorough answers. My therapist said that we should do about three sessions using EMDR, and that if at any time, I felt anxious, we could stop. So, our next three sessions were scheduled and on I went to explore EMDR using my experience of the surgery trauma.

Following each session, I did start to feel better in terms of less anxiety. I was able to get on with my days of work, social events, and general life things. I continued therapy for about three months, and over this period, my anxiety had waned to the point of not being overly worried about things. And this continued for the next three years. I was experiencing less anxiety and my life was more emotionally stable. I was still sitting near doors, but I think that became more of a learned behavior. As a person with anxiety, I learned to cope and if that meant sitting near an exit, then I did. I just thought it was part of my new normal.

## 1998

In 1996, I had finally resigned myself to the fact that working in a group home was not for me any longer. I left the group home after two years and found work in other group homes and even worked for a time at an adolescent shelter. I carried on working odd jobs in my field and continued to find a way to make it work financially. In 1998, I discovered that I wanted to learn more about the field of psychology and maybe even begin to help others in a different setting.

I enrolled in graduate school in 1998 to obtain a master's degree in counseling psychology. Yes, I would need to return to the classroom, but I figured it had been a few years, I should be better right? Suffice it to say, I was not entirely better, at least physically. And I had learned so much about sitting near exits or leaving class early if I felt overly anxious. Graduate school would be okay.

The classrooms were a bit more manageable in grad school mainly because we did more group work and role playing. Sure, there were lectures where I would sit for an hour and listen to the professor, but it was manageable. Grad school was different. I wish I could explain that in a more effective way, but grad school was more relaxed.

I was still experiencing some issues with feeling the need to escape, and even when I had to get up, no one cared. The other students were getting up during class too! Maybe undergrads are more compliant and will stay seated until the end of the class, or maybe this was just my perception. All I know was I did feel more relaxed.

During grad school, I worked for a large nonprofit providing in-home education services to parents whose children had been removed by the courts. I did not have any issues with this job, as I worked primarily in the field. It was a good job and taught me so much about how the social service system works.

But sometime in 1998, the anxiety returned with a vengeance. School did not appear to be the issue because I only went two nights a week, and I was more relaxed in that context. I am not sure to this day why the anxiety returned, but it did.

I had met someone in 1997 who would later become my second husband, but I know he was not the cause of my returning to the excessive worry and needing to escape once again. I was using all available resources to help me, but nothing was working. And then by some miracle, I found out why.

When one enters grad school, getting therapy

is a requirement. I guess they want to make sure you

are emotionally well enough to start working with

clients during the internship portion of the program.

I found a therapist that would not only help me with

the school requirement, but she was also willing to

help me with getting internship hours for my degree.

I was so relieved! Two birds and all.

After a couple of sessions with this new therapist, she asked about prior drug or alcohol issues. I explained my seven dark years of addiction to cocaine, and she said something to me that would again change my life forever. Seems that when we abuse substances, our brain chemistry will never be the same as it was pre-drug use. She explained that this could have something to do with the development of an anxiety disorder. The drugs had rewired my brain chemistry, and it was possible that neurotransmitters such as dopamine and serotonin were not working as they should. It does make sense even today.

She also suggested that I try an antidepressant medication to help with the anxiety, and to follow up with my physician. After a lengthy consultation with my doctor, I was prescribed Paxil. The doctor also suggested that I follow up with a gastrointestinal specialist to see if there were any lingering physical effects of the gallbladder removal. I explained that my surgery was six years prior, and he stated, the effects of that surgery can last years or even over one's lifetime.

I think I was on information overload, but it was such a relief to get answers. I immediately followed up with a GI specialist and did discover that some individuals who have their gallbladders removed have issues with how food is processed. I am not going to get all technical here because I am not sure how this works, but again it made sense.

One of the issues directly related to my anxiety disorder were the physical symptoms. As you might recall, early on I had the bowling alley panic attack followed by a couple of years of trying to escape classrooms. Since anxiety manifests in such different ways, and with symptoms being as unique as we are, I will share one of the most distressing symptoms I experienced with anxiety.

Part of the reason I needed to escape the confines of a classroom, or some other enclosed space was due to my feeling like I was going to explode. Not literally, but more figuratively. Explode in terms of my digestive tract. I was either going to hurl chunks or make a mess of my pants. What I know about anxiety today is that anxious feelings begin with a thought. Typically, we are not aware of these thoughts, but they do occur. Thoughts are the precursor to our feelings and emotions. So, I would start to feel my stomach and bowels churning, and the thought was, I am going to embarrass myself in this classroom or conference room and make a mess of everything. This though would fuel the anxiety and make it worse. The feelings were amplified by this thought, until I had no other recourse but to flee the situation and head straight to the restroom.

Now, moving back to what the GI specialist told me and how food is processed post gallbladder surgery. Usually before class I would eat dinner. Mainly because I had to sit in a classroom for 3-4 hours but also because I needed to eat. Well, if I now process food differently, then maybe the stomach gurgles and subsequent anxiety were related to that. It did make quite a bit of sense. I did notice that if I didn't eat or maybe just had a small nibble of something, that the anxiety was lessened. Maybe there was a connection between the gallbladder surgery and my anxiety after all! I now had a physical reason for the anxiety and my need to escape.

Physical symptoms can certainly heighten anxious feelings. But at that time, I had no idea that could cause anxiety. I did at the very least have some answers to my chronic diarrhea and constant GI upset for all those years. Even today, my stomach may gurgle after a meal, or I might have to use the restroom after breakfast, but I am 100% okay with that because there is a physical connection. And really, I have learned to deal with that by often adjusting what I eat by where I am going next. It no longer creates anxiety, but rather a sense of, okay, that is what I need to do. Even after all these years, I still can get an upset system just by the foods I eat particularly sugary foods. So, when in doubt, I do try to avoid these foods.

# First Brief Recap

Within this first section, reasons were provided on how I believed generalized anxiety developed for me. I think it is safe to assume that the reasons were specific to my experiences and my biological, social, and psychological makeup. What does all of it really mean and how can this information benefit you?

I think through sharing this information, you might see something that relates to you. Maybe then you can look for the reasons why you could have developed an anxiety disorder. Again, some folks need to know the reasons, and others do not. I do not focus too much on the reasons why, but in a way, it does help to put things in perspective. I do kind of like to have more information than not enough.

Most of the information shared thus far does focus on several biological causes of my anxiety, but again, we are all different, and my experiences will be different from yours. Do I believe that I developed generalized anxiety because of the drug use, surgery, and subsequent trauma? Yes. But I also believe that there were other considerations. As previously mentioned, the bio/psycho/social model is one way to look at who we are. We simply cannot leave out looking at our psychological and social factors as well. I will now shift to my social and psychological design that could also align with the development of an anxiety disorder.

# My Social and Psychological Models

After reading the previous pages, does anything strike you as interesting as related to an anxiety disorder and one's psychological and social worlds? I can see some relationship between not liking conflict, being the mascot in my family, and people pleasing for the catalyst to developing an anxiety disorder. I can also see needing to hide emotions at all costs. These are mostly psychological factors, which I will review later. For now, let me focus on a few social issues.

My social makeup is quite diverse, but this is the lens I see myself through today. I enjoy quiet days, and I also enjoy socializing. In prior years though, I see someone different. Up until high school, I was very social and had many friends. High school was not an ideal experience for me. I had few friends and was socially isolated. I did not even get asked to any social events such as homecoming, except for one dance as a sophomore. I stayed home on most weekend nights quietly keeping to myself and watching movies. When I look back on my high school years, what I see is sadness and worthlessness. I felt like I was not as good as others who were more popular. I constantly compared myself to them and never felt like I measured up. If I could sum up high school, the overarching feeling was, at least I graduated!

When I started college, I had a better experience, but I was still comparing myself to others. I was a member of a fraternal organization, and I had my first boyfriend, who was quite popular. We had fun and went to many parties. I do remember though at one party, I sat in the corner and mentally compared myself to everyone in the room. I thought, I am not as pretty as her, or as smart as him. It did not matter the gender either. These comparisons crossed gender lines. During one party, I had an overwhelming feeling of needing to escape. Now mind you, this was way before the drug use and the surgery.

As a psychology professional, I do know there is a relationship between generalized anxiety and low self-esteem. Because we are human, we face acceptance as well as rejection all the time. The way we evaluate this acceptance and rejection can influence how we feel about ourselves. But we are seeing something that might not even be there. Some people are quite adept at handling acceptance and rejection, and others like me, place a price tag on this acceptance and rejection and allow it to change how we feel about ourselves.

Let's go back to the party and see what was really going on. Comparing myself to everyone else in the room was my way of evaluating others and how I measured up. What I was ultimately doing was misreading that acceptance and rejection to the point where it affected my self-worth. I knew that people at this party liked me, as I was a part of this group. I knew this on a conscious level. But what I thought and felt was quite different. This foundation of miscalculating the situation as it was versus what I thought it was, could have played a role in the development of my anxiety disorder. Not to mention, at this party, I started feeling anxious. Like I needed to escape the party to calm down! I believe this was the first time I experienced any anxiety-related symptoms.

Three years later when I started using cocaine, I was accepted and liked by everyone around me. Why? Because I knew how to get the good stuff, and I was quite the party animal. Now would I have been so social without the boost of a stimulant? Probably not. And that is one thing that I understand now about drug use. It alters us in so many ways—socially as well as psychologically and physically.

During my heavy metal years, I was the one who got the drugs for our trips to concerts out of state. Again, well liked. Of course, that is one way to look at it! I am not sure even to this day if those "friends" liked me or the drugs. Today, I do not give it any thought, but it does provide more foundation.

After I stopped using drugs in 1991, I continued to be social, and my friends were truly my friends. In the mid and late 1990s, I was very social. I lived in Huntington Beach after all, and I had many friends. I was starting to feel more worthy, but I do recall still comparing myself to others. But these comparisons were more related to others who had better jobs or a nicer apartment and less about other things. After meeting my now spouse in 1997, I continued to be social and rather enjoyed myself quite a bit. My phone was constantly ringing with invitations to events and gatherings, and I did have fun. But that nagging evaluation of my worth versus the worth of others was something I grappled with daily.

Now I will review my psychological makeup and how who I was and how I behaved could have influenced the development and maintenance of my anxiety disorder.

As a young child, I constantly looked for the approval of others. I wanted so much to be liked and to be the one in the family that resolved any tension or conflicts through story telling and making jokes. Ah, the mascot role! Even to this day, I can still see this part of myself.

I tried to be the best student, the best friend, and the best sister. I am not sure why this was important for me; I just knew it was. The joke telling at the dinner table was my way of resolving tension that others might be experiencing. At a young age, I was not quite sure if this perceived tension was real, or if it was something else. All I knew was I did not like how it felt. Suffice it to say that this role of the mascot carried with me throughout adolescence and into young adulthood.

The attempts at trying so desperately to get others to like me extended into relationships as well. If you recall, I attempted to keep my first love with me through feigning pregnancy or wanting to hurt myself. Such desperation to avoid feelings of rejection. In a manner of speaking, I also used men to help me feel worthwhile. And I suppose drugs allowed me to be someone that I truly was not. Drugs can reduce inhibitions, and I was after all, the life of many parties!

The idea of being a people pleaser is not a new concept. I think it is present in most individuals who experience addiction, and as a human, of course we naturally want to be liked by others. But often this desire extends beyond normal limits. To what extent though is pleasing others normal versus abnormal?

This is a difficult question to answer really. I believe that if you care what others think, that is normal. After all, sociopaths generally do not care what people think about them. But as normal citizens, we do care. Again, human nature is more geared toward acceptance from others.

The issue becomes difficult to assess when we start looking at individual behavior and what lengths we might go through to be accepted. I think that is how we assess the normality of acceptance. In my experience as a young adult, feigning pregnancy or wanting to harm myself in some way was how I believed I needed to behave for someone to accept me. There are some folks that would have simply walked away from that relationship and moved forward. Maybe others would have done worse.

But is this want of acceptance related to an anxiety disorder? You bet it is. In each of us, I believe we have what are known as core beliefs. These beliefs are unique to us and based on our experiences. I see core beliefs as an algorithm, or an instructional guide to how we behave. Maybe if you have been to therapy, you might have heard your therapist mention core beliefs. They are rather important. A core belief is something that probably originated in childhood, but it is something that you carry with you. Core beliefs dictate how we feel about ourselves and can influence your sense of value or worth as a person.

My core belief is I am worthless. I am not sure how this originated, but it has been the guiding instruction for how I behave. This is something I have been working on for years. If this core belief originated in childhood, then this lack of self-worth has affected my behavior. Again, how does anxiety fit into this? I will share my perspective.

My lack of self-worth influenced my behavior. Using the example of my first boyfriend and feigning pregnancy, etc., I would hazard a guess that I behaved that way because I felt worthless and not worthy of love from this person. If he did not want me, then that just solidifies that I am worthless. It connected straight to my core belief. Maybe at that time I was experiencing anxiety, and I just did not understand what it was.

Since anxiety captures us at our core and affects all areas, it can also take our sense of worth as a person. It is beginning to sound like the chicken and egg scenario, isn't it? Which came first? If the core belief came first, as I believed it did, then that core belief also could have been the precipitating factor of developing an anxiety disorder. At least on a psychological level. In essence, having a diminished sense of self-worth, might have allowed the anxiety to develop.

Once the anxiety cycle began, I became a self-fulfilling prophecy. I experience an anxious situation or feel anxiety in my body, and I start to think, see I am inadequate or worthless. The anxiety confirms my core believe. I cannot even handle this situation or these feelings inside. And, if I don't behave a certain way, others will see my worthlessness, which in turn perpetuates that core belief.

As the family mascot, always trying so hard to relieve tension, I believe my anxiety had a solid foundation in which to develop. Family mascots in my opinion are people pleasers, forever attempting to make everyone happy. Life is so much better when people laugh, and tension disappears!

But people pleasing also allows anxiety to grow within us. Truth is, we are never really able to lessen all the tension experienced by a family or at work. People pleasing also comes down to more feelings of inadequacy. Why can't I make everything better? With all these demands that I constantly put on myself growing up, no wonder I developed an anxiety disorder!

Let's switch gears for a moment. Most of what was presented above goes from left to right—childhood to disorder. But turn that around. The anxiety also exacerbates the people pleasing and sense of worthlessness. When I experienced my panic attack at the bowling alley, I had thoughts of what is wrong with me. I must be crazy! I cannot even control my emotions or how I feel. I therefore must be worthless. People pleasing can also influence the continuation of anxious symptoms. What it does is contribute to my worry of not being liked or upsetting others. And what is anxiety mostly related to? Worry. Not to mention, if I am spending my time worrying about what others think of me, then I am not thinking about how I feel. I am putting everything but me first. This is an exhaustive cycle and when I think of this now, it really does help to

explain how my anxiety has fueled my people

pleasing behavior. If I am constantly trying to please

others and putting others' needs before my own,

then where do I fit in? How can I help myself? I

cannot share my anxious feelings with anyone

because it will show I am weak. It would be better to

just let everyone know that I am fine. Even though

on the inside my feelings of worthlessness and

needing to please others is still there, driving my

behavior and influencing my anxiety disorder.

## The Year 2000 and Beyond

Moving beyond the possible causes of my anxiety disorder, I would now like to venture into the new millennium. The last 22 years have been interesting to say the least in terms of my anxiety and recovery.

Remembering all the way back to the year 2000, I seem to recall that many of us were up in arms about the new century. The banks, the airlines, and mostly everyone else was worried about what would happen with our technology once the clock struck midnight on December 31, 1999. But all was well and here we are.

In 2000, I did marry for the second time, and after 22 years, all is well there too! Trust when I say, my husband has been my rock; my super support system that has loved and cared for me through so much. The greatest advice I have for anyone who experiences anxiety, depression, substance abuse, or a myriad of other issues, have a support system. You cannot recover alone!

The beginning of our marriage was great. We got our own townhouse, a couple of cats, and lived a rather routine existence. In 2001, that began to change.

I received my first master's degree in 2001, and like most people do, they try to find new employment when an advanced degree is received. So, I did. I went to work as a social worker, and at first, I thought it would be a good job. The money was good, the benefits were great, but the work itself was hard. I ended up working long hours, seven days a week. It was an all-consuming job that seemed to have no end. I was completely stressed, not sleeping well, and feeling overwhelmed every day.

Even with everything that I knew about

emotions and how to manage them, I was doing a

horrible job at emotional management. Being 100%

overwhelmed every day, I needed some way to reset

and recharge. Around this time, online gambling

became quite popular.

What does one do who feels overwhelmed

and has addiction issues? They gamble online. It was

easy and I could do it from home. What a great way

to deny my overwhelming feelings and anxiety! But I

found once I started, I could not stop. I gambled

online for the next seven years.

I spent money I did not have and spent those seven years in a constant state of anxious denial. My husband knew about it but said nothing. I knew that he knew what I was doing but I got really good at hiding it. Then one day in June 2008, June 24th to be exact, I could not contain any more deceit. I had what one would call an epiphany. Kind of like I did when I stopped using drugs. I had hocked my car and my diamond wedding ring, and once again did some things I was not proud of. There is a scene in the movie "Flight" with Denzel Washington, where he mentions that he could not hold another lie. I know exactly what he means. In 2008, I was physically and psychologically unable to hold in all the turmoil. When I started talking to my husband, it all just came out. I felt like a dam that could no longer hold water.

It all just rushed out in words that I am sure were somewhat incomprehensible. But I got it all out. It was a relief and I actually felt 50 pounds lighter.

After a few days, my husband and I started working on a recovery plan. See, great support from him! He was actually working with me on a recovery plan. As we talked about debt, and what needed taking care of financially, I was blessed with another form of support. My mother-in-law was a big part of the initial path to recovery.

Today I am 13+ years gambling free. When I broke through the denial and started my path to recovery, there were numerous occasions when I felt anxious. I am certain that most in recovery do experience some anxiety simply because there is this what now scenario.

My what now was getting busy working and leading

a productive fulfilling life. We were living in Southern

California at the time, and within a few days of

releasing seven years of gambling to my husband, I

was laid off from my job. The anxiety seemed to

return with a vengeance and there were times when

I felt I could not handle anything else. Recovery is

hard enough, but to lose a job I had had for five

years just added to the feelings of overwhelm and

anxiety.

At the same time all of this was going on, my sister had told me that she had a house in Arizona that we could rent for next to nothing. We would have to move to Arizona naturally, but after 20 years in California, I thought I could be ready for a change. Not to mention paying $1,600 per month for a 500-square foot apartment in California was not conducive to recovering financially from seven years of problem gambling.

Also, my sister had a lead on a job for me working in a hospital as a Nursing Assistant. This required three weeks of paid training, but it was a job. Now, any major change can be stressful, and I believe moving and job changes are in the top 10 of stressful events, but despite feeling completely anxious about moving and starting on a new career path, I did it anyway.

I knew that three weeks of training would be in a classroom setting, so the anxiety was overwhelming when I thought of having to sit in a classroom again. No worries though; sit near the door. And remember, these are nurses and nursing students so by design they would understand anxiety or needing to use the bathroom or even leaving the room because the walls were closing in. For the most part I was right in my assessment.

In January of 2009, I made the move to Arizona, and started the Nursing Assistant training program. My husband followed a couple of months later. He too was going to complete the Nursing Assistant training program at a later time.

When I started working as a Nursing Assistant, I did not realize how demanding the job would be. It was 12-hour shifts, 7 p.m. to 7 a.m., three days a week. I was exhausted. In terms of my anxiety, it was somewhat elevated during this time. Often, I would be in a patient's room, and I would need to leave feeling a sense of dread. I managed to keep it together though, but after six months, I determined that this was not the job for me. I honestly do not know how nurses do this day in and day out for years. My hat is certainly off to all nurses! I have such respect for them.

When I knew I wanted to work in a different field, my friend suggested that I apply at the university where she worked. I did and was employed again for an online university. I could end the story here about life in Arizona, but alas, I cannot because I have an anxiety disorder. Change is part of life and most people do fine with change, but what I have found is that those with an anxiety disorder struggle emotionally with change. The worry, the what ifs, the unfamiliar, and the feelings of panic and dread, are present most days and change is not something that is openly accepted.

The new job itself had many positives such as my own working space, normal business hours, and health benefits. But I did little to think about those things. What I focused on were the negative aspects of the job. And these mostly centered around the number of meetings I would need to attend. Meetings with lots of people in huge conference rooms. See where this is going? Overwhelming anxiety! People, closed rooms, and no possible escape. My worst nightmare.

At least three times per week there was a meeting. A team huddle, an operations meeting, or some other hell that I would need to endure. It was almost as if my brain could not handle all the what ifs related to these meetings. My focus became the meetings, the rooms, the doors, the people. Argh, I was making myself crazy!

I tried very hard to endure each meeting counting down the seconds until it was over. I would carry a notebook to each of these meetings, and I found that if I doodled during the meeting, it would help relieve some of the anxiety. But on several occasions the meeting leader would ask me what I was writing because notes were not necessary. Thank you for that! Not only am I sitting here in agony, but then you find it necessary to single me out in front of all these people? Let's just add a layer to the anxiety I was already experiencing, shall we?

Since I liked the job, I wanted to make these

meetings work, and to help myself prior to the

meeting. I would take deep breaths, and maybe if

super anxious, I might even need to pop a Xanax;

small dose mind you. Enough to chill me out. The

meetings did become bearable, but most were

agonizing. I always sat near an exit and would

request the door be left open because it was stuffy

or hot. I did this for two years. Then a surprising

change occurred. I was allowed to work from home.

Oh joy, I could do meetings virtually and not have to

endure the anxiety for all the meetings I was

expected to attend.

Working from home did help with lowering my anxiety levels, but after looking back, I realize it was just a fix. A band aid if you will. Despite all the medications, treatments, counseling, deep breaths, exercise, diet changes, etc. I still experienced generalized anxiety. I knew at some point I would need to take control of this and truly learn to help myself.

The years passed in Arizona, most of them

uneventful and honestly, working from home I was

feeling calmer about life and other things. But the

thing about anxiety is this. Actually, the thing about

most physical or emotional problems is this.

Symptoms come and go. You have good days and

you have not so great days. I always believed that

having a mental health disorder meant that that was

just the way you have learned to cope with life. You

might be anxious, depressed, or abuse a substance

to cope. Hey, life is and can be overwhelming. Let's

face it. Each of us copes in our own way.

My coping mechanism in a way is anxiety. It was my go-to emotion when I would want to deny my true feelings, or not wish to face life in general. If I was feeling anxious, I would get attention, and it would take away the other feelings of low self-worth and it would give me purpose. That might sound odd, but anxiety to me kind of kept me protected from others and the outside world. It was almost like a drug. That does sound odd, but if you have experienced anxiety, you might know what I am referring to. With that, let's move forward into 2018 and beyond.

# 2018 to 2020

I wanted to focus some on this period of time

because some fairly significant changes occurred in

my professional and personal life. And these changes

brought about increased anxiety.

I was working full-time at an online university, actually the same university that I had worked since 2009. But since receiving my PhD in 2015, I was able to teach there on a part-time basis. And I was also working at another online university part-time as an adjunct faculty. I was still working at home, which for someone with anxiety related to in-person meetings and team huddles, continued to work well for me. I had my own bathroom. As described earlier, my anxiety did have a physiological component, accompanied by gastrointestinal distress. So, the bathroom was next door to my office, and no one used it but me. Glorious!

For the last 10 years or so, I have maintained an online journal. I keep notes about family, feelings, work, and personal things that I am experiencing on any given day. Looking back on 2018, and reading the pages of this journal, I recall much sadness. I think I was either bored or just unsure of the future. I do believe there is a connection between depression and anxiety and feeling unsure about life and other things can exacerbate both feelings of sadness and anxiousness. I wrote in 2018 that I felt stuck and incredibly negative most hours of the day.

There existed within me at this time, feelings

of apathy, uncertainty, and worry. Oh, the worry!

The chief component of anxiety. I think it was mainly

due to not knowing what I wanted in terms of

satisfying work. Now I love teaching and working

online because I really have met some interesting

people. And teaching them about psychology and

helping them achieve academic success is truly a

great job experience for me.

But I was thinking about other endeavors.

What would I love to do more than anything? First,

open an animal shelter, but also, I wanted to write

professionally. I love writing and can write for hours.

Stories, my journal, even my task list! I just love

writing. I was positive that I could write a blog or a

Facebook page every day and get traffic. What I

discovered was that I was too focused on who

responded while not about developing my writing

skills. I did take a break from writing for a couple of

years, but now I am back writing books.

Reflecting on the first few months of 2018, I found I wrote much about continued sadness, and that sadness was related mostly to work. I did start a new job in March of 2018, and I still hold that job today. Things were looking up and I was not bored or sad much any longer.

April 2018 was a bizarre month for me emotionally, and the anxiety was overwhelming. I planned a trip to Seattle with my husband for my nephew's 30th birthday. I hate flying so as soon as I booked the flight, the anxiety started to overwhelm me. Thoughts of dying, thoughts of crashing, and all the what ifs that accompany feeling anxious. By the way, a day after we flew home from Seattle, there was a plane incident on the same airline that I flew the day before. It confirmed my anxiety. See, people die on airplanes, they are not safe despite statistics and everyone telling you it is safer than driving, blah, blah, blah. That was the anxiety talking! So much worry about nothing! Right? Well, I still have problems getting on airplanes, but I will fly if I absolutely need to, but I prefer not to.

As summer of 2018 approached, I started to feel overwhelming anxiety again. I think it was related to the hot weather and the start of our monsoon season here in Arizona. It can get really hot here and then the thunderstorms start. I have never liked thunderstorms! All the noise and the lightning flashes. Not to mention, the storms can be fairly scary. And scary equals massive anxiety for someone like me. Our monsoon season usually starts in July and does not let up until late August. Two months of anxiety and fear! At least it gives me something to look forward to each year. I used to think that I had a phobia related to storms, and a phobia of flying, but phobias typically involve avoidance. I do not and have not avoided these two areas of my life. I just experience dread, anxiety, and fear when faced with storms or flying.

During July and August of 2018, there was tremendous anxiety because of the storms I experienced. I specifically wrote in my journal on July 6, 2018, the monsoons will start in a few days, and I am already feeling anxious. Followed by, I need to get a grip on this. On July 17, 2018, I wrote that I had a meltdown. The day prior there were these dark ominous clouds off to the east, and I remember thinking, wow, those clouds are really black. I went into my office, put on my headphones, and anticipated fear and anxiety. And lo and behold, that is what happened. I had an emotional meltdown, the first of many that would follow over the next two years.

The meltdowns are an experience to say the least. First it begins with what if thoughts that are so overwhelming that I feel like I will jump out of my skin. Often, I want to scream—STOP IT! But that does not help. Next are the shaky hands, heart palpitations, and sweating. And then, if that weren't enough, I start to uncontrollably sob. And not just sobbing, but deep belly sobbing. The kind where your stomach hurts afterward. When this happens, I do have the loving arms of a great husband to let me know that everything will be okay and to breathe! After 20 minutes or so, I do start to feel better, and soon after that, the storm has subsided.

This was followed by several more meltdowns over the next week. We did have many storms during the first few weeks of July 2018, and some were really bad. All I wrote in my journal was, this sucks so bad.

In early August 2018, I ended up in the emergency room because of my heart palpitations. Turns out, I was okay physically. I was prescribed Ativan for anxiety, and I went about my day. I was required to have a follow up with a cardiologist just to be sure though. And, after the consultation with the cardiologist, I discovered that physically, I was okay. All tests normal.

The remainder of 2018 was fairly normal, at least for me. I was able to recover from the heart palpitations and it appeared that autumn was on its way. Meaning, no more storms. But there was still anxiety. My husband and I were planning a trip in the fall, and we were going to visit friends in Indiana and family in Ohio. And yes, this trip involved an airplane and me getting on said airplane and flying for a few hours. The obsessive thoughts about flying started about three weeks before we were scheduled to travel.

When I say obsessive thoughts and worry, I mean constant thoughts each and every waking hour of every day. I even thought that I should cancel the flights without telling my husband, and then when we arrived at the airport, wow, are flights were cancelled. How did that happen? Whatever it took to not fly! I was desperate. How could I protect myself and relieve my anxiety about this trip? Simple, don't go. Make something up. Too much work, not the right time, etc. We ended up not going on this trip because on the day we were scheduled to leave, another meltdown. It reminded me of that scene in Rain Man where Dustin Hoffman's character freaks out at the airport. That was me.

I was happy we were not going, and I did not have to fly, but I was also ashamed for letting my husband down. He really wanted to go on this trip. As long as I didn't have to go, in my mind, everything was okay. Each time I gave into the anxiety and canceled plans and trips, I was okay. The anxiety subsided.

For the remainder of 2018, life was normal. I didn't have anything planned and that was just fine with me. Stormy season was over, and I did not have to travel anywhere. Life was good!

In 2019 I noticed something that I think I obsessed about at that time. Maybe I still do in a way, but I do think this has something to do with my anxiety. When you live in a world of constant what ifs, and question all that is happening, and fear that is overwhelming, often it can be challenging to be organized. I discovered that the first few months of 2019 was all about getting myself organized. I worked a couple of jobs after all, and many weeks it was difficult to remember what I had done and what I needed to do.

At the start of the year, I would often experience mini panic attacks, because I just did not know how I was going to do all the work that I needed to do. Funny thing though, I was able to get it all done regardless of how I had it organized. So, when I say I obsess about organization, I mean every day I go to Amazon to find the perfect organizer. There was a perfect planner out there for me that would work and that would finally get me organized. I now realize that no such thing exists! I must have 20 planners in my closet gathering dust.

Because of feeling overwhelmed and anxious about being organized, sometimes I would not work at all. And the following day would feel depressed that I did not work on anything. In a minor way, I still think today about being organized. I imagine that it has something to do with the little hamster running around in my head running on his metal wheel and getting absolutely nowhere no matter how fast he would run. That is how a person feels when anxious and unorganized.

In February 2019, I was called to jury duty and since it was not called off, I had to go. So here we go again with sitting in a packed room where the doors seemed to be closed shut and sealed with super glue. I had no escape route. So many people, so much anxiety. What if I passed gas or had to use the bathroom? Fortunately, nothing happened for the first few hours, but those hours seemed like days, and I was doing everything in my power to shut my brain off. At the lunch break, a few of the other potential jurors went to a local restaurant and had food. I was not sure if I should eat or not because I knew I would feel anxious afterward sitting in a cramped courtroom waiting to be called. After we finished with lunch, I had an anxiety attack. I was walking around the halls of the courthouse going in and out of the bathroom. I had eaten next to nothing

so it couldn't have been the food. After about half an

hour, I ended up walking into the courtroom late and

had to sit somewhere without a door nearby.

As people were being called to be questioned

by the judge and attorneys, I would move to their

seat if they were closer to an exit. I did this for two

hours until the remaining potential jurors were

excused, which included me. I could not wait to get

home.

The year progressed and for the first few months of that year, I experienced worry that was overwhelming. And I had no basis for this worry. I was not sleeping well constantly worrying about everything. I worried about the weather, my cats, work, finances, and whatever else I could jam into my brain. And I was worrying about the Arizona monsoon season that was not even due for another few months.

And with all that I worried about for the first few months of the year; I had a new worry in April. My husband and I were planning a trip to Ohio and Indiana to see family and friends. We were not scheduled to leave until June, but already the overwhelming anxiety of flying was starting. I found myself praying so hard that my husband would change his mind about the trip, and we would just stay home. I think my husband was picking up on my anxiety about flying though and said we could take the train. I was thrilled! No flying for me!

The trip was great! Eleven days, most of

which was spent on the train. But that part was

good. Trains do not fall out of the sky! During the trip

I did have a couple of meltdowns, and not sure even

to this day what those were about. I spent most of

my vacation thinking about work and worrying about

other stuff. My little hamster was still running wild

on his little metal wheel even on vacation.

And the hamster kept running too! It was that time of year in Arizona. The summer monsoons were on the way. And yes, I usually started worrying about the possibility of storms months before they were scheduled to arrive. I obsessed about the weather and would spend hours looking at predictions for the upcoming monsoon season. Was it going to be a stormy season, or would I get some reprieve and it would be a lighter storm season? Every time I saw a cloud, my heart would start racing and my mind would go in all kinds of direction. Is that a storm, is that cloud going to turn black, will it thunder? What will I do?

When I look back now on the remainder of 2019, I see worry, constant worry. About finances, work, storms, and whatever else my mind conjured up. I do not recall meltdowns or panic attacks, but I did spend an inordinate amount of time trying to organize myself once again on paper. Computer calendar, handwritten calendar, task list, etc. Which was really going to get me organized? And then in December 2019, I started hearing on the news that a flu bug was making its rounds overseas. Wonder what that is about?

## 2020 and 2021

This year gets its own heading and I know you know why. It was a difficult year for millions of people. Since most of us experienced this year and the year that followed differently, I won't go into much detail here.

Most of 2020 was a blur. Starting in March 2020, I do remember not wanting to leave the house. When we went to the grocery store, it felt like an episode of the Walking Dead. It was surreal. Masks, social distancing, etc. were becoming our normal. When we left the grocery store, I cried. I said, we are social beings, we are supposed to be around people! As bad as the virus was and is, I now know that it was necessary for us to stay apart from others and to wear a mask. I do recall not worrying so much about things in my life during 2020. There were bigger fish to fry!

In my personal world though, a couple of things did occur in 2020 that were substantial. First, in February 2020, I was outside feeding the birds in my backyard, and I noticed a little black and white cat on the ground under a tree. I called to the cat, and it hissed at me! I decided to leave the cat some food, and I watched it gobble it up. Okay, she is obviously a stray or maybe even semi-feral. I kept feeding her (discovered she is she), and over the course of the next few months, I was able to get her on our front porch. I would sit on a bench with her, and over time I was able to pet her. We named her Ruby Lipbaum, but before we knew she was she, we called it Irv Goldman. We love being creative with names.

With 2020 being a mostly lockdown year, it was nice to have Ruby to spend time with and to train her to become our pet cat. It kept the boredom at bay, and in retrospect, she really saved me in some small way. I was able to help a cat during the pandemic and long story short, she is 100% our cat now. She sleeps with me, and she has her own special blankets to sleep on. It was a challenging experience getting her in the house, and around our other cats. They are not best friends by any stretch of the imagination, but they tolerate each other. It took many months to get Ruby to where she is now, but I am very patient when it comes to animals. And she really did help with my anxiety. I felt so calm around her, and my focus was all on her and becoming our pet. I guess sometimes you need a distraction from life and other things.

The year 2020 offered another relief so to speak of feeling anxious. Sometime in 2020, and I cannot remember the month as most of that year is a blur, my husband began to experience chronic belching. And I do not mean a healthy release after drinking a carbonated beverage or a large meal, I mean belching consistently and constantly for hours on end. He tried everything to relieve this, and nothing seemed to work.

At some point he visited his general practitioner, and no real solution was provided. Some days he belched all day, and other days it was manageable. I thought it was stress related to the pandemic. My husband is a very social person, and I am convinced the lockdown etc. provided a stressor for him.

Not only was my husband having belching issues, but he was also starting to feel his heartbeat loudly along with a racing mind. He was so animated and many days it was challenging to focus on my work. He would talk very quickly and talk about how he was feeling. I certainly would never discount anyone who wanted to share their feelings; however, my husband shared each twinge, belch, etc. that he felt. It was a bit much on some days. He even woke me up at 3:00 a.m. once to talk about how he was feeling. Again, I would listen to him naturally. It is what one does for their husband!

We did start to talk about the possibility of him experiencing anxiety, and I remember the first thing I said was, go get some help. He did and over time he started to feel better. I bring up this for one reason only. When you have an anxiety, how do you help someone else who is now experiencing anxiety as well? The short answer is, it was easy for me because I could empathize. I knew exactly what he was going through, and I had some tools he could use. So now, two people in the same home with an anxiety disorder! It is certainly not an issue for either of us. I think in fact it might have brought us closer emotionally. He understands now how I feel, and I can certainly appreciate how he feels. And we make it a daily point to talk and share our feelings on a daily basis. Not too shabby!

The next year, 2021, was also challenging but for different reasons. I did wish that 2021 would be better than 2020. And, in many ways, it was. There was a vaccine available, and things seemed to be improving somewhat. But there was something else that occurred in 2021 that really helped me in a way with my anxiety.

In 2021, there were a couple of family members that started to exhibit symptoms of depression and hopelessness. I was curious about this because neither family member had exhibited any signs of depression prior. When I think about this today, I am convinced this had something to do with the pandemic. These two family members were truly the social ones in the family, and it must have been so difficult to not be able to do the things they liked to do. Travel was limited, time spent with friends and family was limited, and these two individuals were not very happy about being confined to places like their homes.

This did not help me per se with my anxiety, but it did open my eyes to a global truth. So many people were experiencing symptoms of depression and anxiety since the beginning of the pandemic, and I was starting to feel normal in some ways. I am by no means discounting others by saying that I felt normal. My anxiety did have good days and bad days throughout 2021, and I am sure others had and have good days and bad days as well. What I mean by normal is I was able to identify with others and how others were feeling. Maybe anxiety is a normal reaction to stress and a reaction when someone feels overwhelmed. I basically just felt like so many others and that to me, is a kind of normalcy.

# Now What or So What

My journey of generalized anxiety continues to present day, and I am 100% okay with that. I do have somewhat of a so what attitude now because I have discovered one very important thing about myself. I am okay!

I still have bad days where feelings of anxiety can overwhelm me, but I am even okay with that.

Generalized anxiety is still not something I have, but something I experience and manage, and that is fine. I have learned acceptance and compassion for myself. I understand the causes and I have a toolbox of great resources that I can draw upon when needed.

My mind is quieter as well. When I find myself saying what if, I stop and say, quit it very loud. I also have a great support system with my husband and other friends and family members. I deep breathe when needed and attempt to reduce negativity in my life. I still don't like thunderstorms or flying, but I am managing that as well. I refuse to let anxiety take my heart, mind, and soul like it has in the past. Through the years, I have learned to accept myself as I am and not let it affect my activities of daily living any longer.

# Final Words

My desire to help others learn about anxiety and start or continue the road to recovery, was the primary motivation for writing this book. I certainly do not have all the answers. But what I do have is a perspective on anxiety that could possibly provide you with support. Knowing that someone shares your journey with anxiety, can also provide hope. A feeling that you are not alone. That others experience similar emotions to you. That we can support each other through understanding and recovery.

As an academic, I have read countless articles on anxiety and treatment. Most of this reading was on a clinical level though, which meant reading through studies on what therapeutic treatment works best for anxiety, what medications are showing great promise, and the list goes on. I am not discounting any of the research on anxiety or recovery because these studies are hugely important to the academic community. Without research, we would not be able to learn new ways of thinking about anxiety. We would not understand how anxiety affects us and influences our activities of daily living. We would not understand what treatments are available and what can help us overcome these debilitating symptoms. Suffice it to say, research is and will continue to be necessary.

Generalized Anxiety Disorder or GAD is a pervasive, and often debilitating mental health issue. If you or someone you know experiences anxiety or was recently diagnosed with GAD, it is my wish this story will help you find understanding and maybe some peace.

My intent was to share my personal journey with you, so you can learn from my experiences. As an academic, I know sharing experiences is a great learning tool. We learn much from listening to others and sharing our stories.

I am not a licensed clinician, but I do have advanced

degrees in psychology and counseling, I know that

anxiety exists for many millions of Americans. The

overwhelming feelings of dread and worry are

consuming, and over time, these feelings begin to

dictate how we live. I also know there are many

trained professionals out there who are willing to

help you. All you have to do is ask.

Maybe this book will help you begin your journey to recovery. To say enough, I need help. Maybe this book is the catalyst for you to begin thinking about GAD in a different way and to recognize that you are not alone. Maybe this book will help you realize that GAD is not specific to certain individuals or those who might be in high-stress jobs or any plethora of other things. GAD affects many who are just like you and me.

And finally, this disorder is real, and no one should ever imply that you experience anxiety because you are weak or too emotional. The stigma associated with mental health issues is becoming less of a concern thanks to all those who have spoken up about their disorder. I encourage this and applaud those who have done so. I do see mental health concerns becoming more mainstream and that is a very good thing. For years, many were thought of as less than or vulnerable if they experienced something like GAD. Let me tell you that I have never felt anything but human in my years with GAD. Having emotions is part of being human.